SOMALIA 2015 HUMAN RIGHTS REPORT

EXECUTIVE SUMMARY

The Federal Government of Somalia, formed in 2012, was led by President Hassan Sheikh Mohamud. Clan elders nominated the members of the House of the People of the Federal Parliament in 2012. Parliament elected Hassan Sheikh Mohamud as president later that year. Former Transitional Federal Government (TFG) president and presidential candidate Sheikh Sharif described the presidential vote as fair and conceded defeat. The regional governments of the self-declared Republic of Somaliland in the northwest and Puntland in the northeast controlled their respective jurisdictions. In July the government established the Interim Galmudug Administration (IGA) in the central part of the country. The IGA, the Interim Juba Administration (IJA), and the Interim South West Administration (ISWA) did not fully control their jurisdictions. The terrorist organization al-Shabaab retained control of some towns and rural areas but by year's end lost control of the key cities of Bardheere and Dinsoor and several other towns and villages in the south and central regions to the African Union Mission in Somalia (AMISOM) and Somali security forces. Civilian authorities did not maintain effective control over the security forces.

Major human rights abuses included killings of civilians by al-Shabaab, Somali security forces, and unknown assailants. Violence and discrimination against women and girls, including rape and female genital mutilation/cutting (FGM/C), were widespread. Civilians did not have the ability to change their government through the ability to vote in free and fair elections.

Other major human rights abuses included disappearance; torture and other cruel, inhuman, or degrading treatment or punishment; harsh and life-threatening prison conditions; arbitrary and politically motivated arrest and detention; denial of fair public trial; use of excessive force and other abuses in internal conflict; restrictions on freedoms of speech and press, assembly and association, religion, and movement; forced eviction and relocation of internally displaced persons (IDPs); diversion of humanitarian assistance; corruption; trafficking in persons; abuse of and discrimination against minority clans and persons with disabilities; social stigmatization of lesbian, gay, bisexual, transgender, and intersex (LGBTI) individuals; restrictions on workers' rights; forced labor; and child labor.

In general impunity remained the norm. Government authorities took minimal steps to prosecute and punish officials who committed abuses, particularly military and police officials accused of committing rape, killings, clan warfare, and extortion of civilians.

Clan militias and al-Shabaab continued to commit grave abuses throughout the country, including extrajudicial killings, disappearances, cruel and unusual punishment, rape, restrictions on civil liberties and freedom of movement, restrictions on nongovernmental organizations (NGOs) and humanitarian assistance, and conscription and use of child soldiers. Al-Shabaab recruited child soldiers. AMISOM troops killed civilians and committed sexual abuse and exploitation, including rape of women and girls.

Section 1. Respect for the Integrity of the Person, Including Freedom from:

a. Arbitrary or Unlawful Deprivation of Life

Government security forces and allied militias, persons wearing uniforms, regional security forces, al-Shabaab, and unknown assailants committed arbitrary or unlawful killings. Government and regional authorities executed persons without due process. Armed clashes and attacks killed civilians (see section 1.g.). Impunity remained the norm.

Federal forces killed protesters (see section 2.b.). For example, on January 1, government forces reportedly fired at Ahlu Sunna Wal Jama'a (ASWJ) supporters violently protesting against the federal government in Galhareeri, Galguduud Region, killing two and injuring others.

Military trials, which sometimes included civilian defendants, often did not afford defendants legal representation or the opportunity to appeal (see also section 1.e.). Federal and regional authorities sometimes executed those sentenced to death within days of the court's verdict, particularly in cases where defendants directly confessed their membership in al-Shabaab before the courts. National figures on executions were unreliable. Human rights organizations questioned the military courts' ability to enforce appropriate safeguards relating to due process, the right to seek pardon, or commutation of sentence as well as to implement sentences in a manner that meets international standards.

On April 13, Somaliland authorities executed by firing squad six persons convicted of murder.

On August 20, a federal military court executed soldier Mohamed Ali Adan after he was convicted of killing another soldier. Human rights organizations expressed concern regarding lack of due process.

On September 18, regional authorities in Kismayo executed seven IJA soldiers hours after a regional military court convicted them of killing two civilians. The accused were denied legal representation.

Al-Shabaab continued to kill civilians (see also sections 1.g., 2.a., and 6). The killings included al-Shabaab's execution of persons it accused of spying for and collaborating with Somali national forces and affiliated militias. For example, on March 21, al-Shabaab executed one man accused of spying for the Ethiopian government in Galhareeri, Galgaduud Region.

Unidentified gunmen also killed persons, including members of parliament, judges, National Intelligence and Security Agency (NISA) agents, Somali National Army (SNA) soldiers, and other government officials, as well as traditional elders and international organization workers, with impunity.

For example, on February 3, unidentified gunmen killed cleric Sheikh Hassan Soor-Madiide in Baidoa, Bay Region, as he exited a local mosque. The motive for the killing remained unknown.

The investigation of the April 2014 assassination of two employees of the UN Office of Drugs and Crime (UNODC) remained incomplete. Clement Bernard Gorrissen, a French citizen, and Simon Davis, a UK citizen, were killed as they disembarked from their plane in Galkayo, Mudug Region.

Fighting among clans and subclans, particularly over water and land resources, resulted in killings and displacements (see section 1.g.). Revenge killings occurred.

On July 4, clashes between Dhulbahante and Habar Yunis clans in Guumeys village, Somaliland, resulted in two deaths and at least four wounded.

b. Disappearance

Al-Shabaab continued to abduct persons, including humanitarian workers (see section 1.g.). Pirates continued to hold persons kidnapped in previous years. There were no reports government authorities committed politically motivated or other disappearances.

On May 13, al-Shabaab fighters kidnapped a reported 14 Iranian fishermen who were allegedly fishing in Somali waters near El-Dheer, Galguduud Region, when their vessel washed ashore.

As of December the International Maritime Bureau noted one incident of piracy in the country during the year, compared with three incidents in 2014 and 15 in 2013.

On February 26, pirates released four Thai hostages whom they had held since 2010 and who were from the fishing vessel Prantalay 12. Twenty-six crewmembers from the Naham 3, captured in 2012, remained in captivity.

On November 22, armed men hijacked the FV Muhammadi, a Pakistani-owned, Iranian-flagged vessel with a crew of 15 Iranians, 200 nautical miles off the coast of Somalia.

c. Torture and Other Cruel, Inhuman, or Degrading Treatment or Punishment

The provisional federal constitution prohibits torture and inhuman treatment. Nevertheless, torture and other cruel, inhuman, or degrading treatment or punishment occurred. The UN Monitoring Group on Somalia and Eritrea (SEMG) reported it received allegations that NISA officials committed torture.

Government forces, allied militia, men wearing uniforms, and AMISOM troops committed sexual violence, including rape (see section 1.g.).

Clan leaders in the Lower Juba Region accused the IJA of committing gross human right violations, including torture. On January 6, local politician Mohamed Aden accused IJA authorities of allowing their security forces to commit rape and torture with impunity.

There were numerous reports federal and regional authorities beat journalists (see section 2.a.).

NISA agents routinely carried out mass security sweeps, despite having no legal mandate to arrest and detain suspects. NISA held detainees for prolonged periods without following due process and mistreated suspects during interrogations. For example, on May 25, NISA agents arrested journalist Ali Abdi "Yare" for allegedly criticizing the government. Ali Yare was kept in detention incommunicado without access to legal counsel for at least a week. He was later released but continued to face harassment from government security authorities.

There were several cases throughout the year of al-Shabaab abusing and imposing harsh punishment on persons in areas under its control. For example, on September 28, al-Shabaab stoned to death a woman accused of adultery in Barawe (see section 6, Women). Al-Shabaab also beheaded three men on September 14, in Yiblan, Hiraan Region, for allegedly being SNA members. Local community members claimed the men were herders and had no association with the armed forces.

Somaliland security forces suppressed supporters of the self-declared Khatumo state in its eastern regions of Sool and Sanaag during the year. The use of force resulted in injuries and internal displacement of persons.

Prison and Detention Center Conditions

Prison and detention center conditions remained harsh and life threatening throughout the country, although Puntland and Somaliland prisons generally provided somewhat better living conditions than prisons in other parts of the country.

Physical Conditions: The number of prisoners and detainees, including juvenile and female prisoners, was unknown. In prisons and detention centers, authorities frequently held juveniles with adults. Authorities often did not separate pretrial detainees from convicted prisoners, particularly in the southern and central regions. The incarceration of juveniles at the request of families who wanted their children disciplined allegedly remained a problem. There continued to be reports of some families sending juveniles from al-Shabaab-controlled areas to prison to prevent al-Shabaab from forcibly recruiting them.

Information on the death rates in prisons and pretrial detention centers was unavailable. Harsh conditions in most prisons and detention centers throughout the country, particularly in the south and central regions and in Mogadishu, included overcrowding and wholly inadequate sanitation, health care, food, water, ventilation, and lighting. Tuberculosis, cholera, and pneumonia were reportedly widespread. Prisoners relied on their families and clans, which often paid the costs associated with detention. In many areas prisoners depended on family members and relief agencies for food.

After a visit to Mogadishu Central Prison in 2013, then prime minister Abdi Farah Shirdon issued a press release calling prison conditions "deplorable" and asked the international community to support long-term improvements to the facility. Mogadishu Central Prison remained the main prison in Mogadishu. According to the UNODC, the prison housed an estimated 1,200 inmates, of whom local authorities estimated 600 were al-Shabaab members or collaborators. A 2012 UN prison assessment noted no adequate separation between juvenile and adult inmates. The UNODC also concluded prisoners' living conditions in Mogadishu Central Prison fell short of meeting minimum international and national standards.

Prison infrastructure across the country remained poor and overcrowded, and it did not permit proper classification and segregation of high-risk detainees. The UNODC continued to assist prison management in establishing a prisoner database to account for inmates and provide for proper separation of detainees.

In 2012 the UN independent expert for Somalia visited several detention centers in Puntland and Somaliland. He found unlawful or arbitrary detentions, such as women and girls detained for disobeying their husbands or parents. He described detention conditions as close to inhuman, stating they were overcrowded and frequently lacked water, sanitation, and ventilation.

Al-Shabaab detained persons in areas under its control in the southern and central regions. Those detained were incarcerated under inhuman conditions for relatively minor "offenses," such as smoking, listening to music, watching or playing soccer, or not wearing a hijab.

Administration: Most prisons did not have ombudsmen, and recordkeeping was inadequate, although some prisons in Somaliland implemented data management systems. There were only limited alternatives to incarceration. Federal law does not specifically allow prisoners to submit complaints to judicial authorities without censorship, although Somaliland law allows prisoners to submit complaints to judicial authorities; according to government officials, prisoners submitted complaints.

Independent Monitoring: Government, Puntland, and Somaliland authorities permitted prison monitoring by independent nongovernmental observers during the year. UNODC representatives visited prisons in Bosaso, Garowe, and Hargeisa several times. UN Assistance Mission in Somalia representatives, other UN organizations, and humanitarian institutions visited prisons throughout the country.

<u>Improvements</u>: UN agencies improved prison facilities in various regions of the country, provided training and mentoring to custodial staff, and implemented vocational training and rehabilitation programs for inmates.

d. Arbitrary Arrest or Detention

The provisional federal constitution prohibits illegal detention. Government security forces and allied militias, regional authorities, clan militias, and al-Shabaab arbitrarily arrested and detained persons.

Role of the Police and Security Apparatus

The provisional federal constitution states that the armed forces are responsible for assuring the country's sovereignty, independence, and territorial integrity and that the national federal and state police are responsible for protecting lives, property, peace, and security. Police were generally ineffective. AMISOM and the SNA worked to maintain order in areas of the southern and central regions. The federal government regularly relied on NISA forces to perform police work, often calling on them to arrest and detain civilians without warrants. Some towns and rural areas in the southern and central regions remained under the control of al-Shabaab and affiliated militias. The Ministry of Defense is responsible for controlling the armed forces. Police forces fall under a mix of local and regional administrations and the government. The national police force remained under the jurisdiction of the Ministry of National Security, while regional authorities maintained police forces falling under their areas' interior or security ministries.

Civilian authorities did not maintain effective control of security forces. Security forces abused civilians and often failed to prevent or respond to societal violence. Authorities rarely investigated abuse by police, army, or militia members, and a culture of impunity was widespread. Authorities sometimes used military courts to try individuals believed to be responsible for abuses. The official ad hoc commissions to investigate abuses by federal military forces and allied militias in the Lower Shabelle Region did not release information regarding the investigation.

The Ministry of Defense's control over the army remained tenuous but somewhat improved with the support of international partners. At year's end the army consisted of approximately 23,000 soldiers, with the bulk of forces located in Middle Shabelle and Lower Shabelle, as well as the Bay, Bakool, and Gedo Regions. The Ministry of Defense exerted greater control over forces in the greater Mogadishu area, extending as far south as Merca, Lower Shabelle Region, west to Baidoa, Bay Region, and north to Jowhar, Middle Shabelle Region. SNA forces consisted of 17 independent brigades. Army forces and progovernment militia operated alongside AMISOM in areas where AMISOM deployed.

Two separate police forces operated in Mogadishu, one under the control of the central government and the other under the Benadir Regional administration. The federal police force maintained its presence in all 17 districts of the capital. Police officers in Mogadishu often owed their positions to clan and familial links rather than to government authorities. AMISOM-formed police units complemented Benadir and federal government policing efforts in Mogadishu. These police officers provided mentoring and advisory support on basic police duties, respect for human rights, crime prevention strategies, community policing, and search procedures. More than 300 AMISOM police officers worked alongside the formed units to provide training to the national police.

Arrest Procedures and Treatment of Detainees

The provisional federal constitution provides for arrested persons to be brought before judicial authorities within 48 hours. The law requires warrants based on sufficient evidence and issued by authorized officials for the apprehension of suspects. The law also provides that arrestees receive prompt notification of the charges against them and judicial determinations, prompt access to a lawyer and family members, and other legal protections. Adherence to these safeguards was rare. The federal government made arrests without warrants and detained individuals arbitrarily. The government sometimes kept high-profile prisoners associated with al-Shabaab in safe houses before officially charging them. The law provides for bail, although courts adhered to this unevenly. Authorities rarely provided indigent persons a lawyer. The government held suspects under house arrest, particularly high-ranking defectors from al-Shabaab with strong clan connections. Security force members and corrupt judicial officers, politicians, and clan elders used their influence to have detainees released.

Arbitrary Arrest: Government and regional authorities arbitrarily arrested and detained numerous persons, including persons accused of terrorism and supporting al-Shabaab. Authorities frequently used allegations of al-Shabaab affiliation to justify arbitrary arrests.

Government, regional authorities, and clan militias arbitrarily arrested journalists (see section 2.a.).

Government forces conducted operations to arrest youths they perceived as suspicious without executing warrants.

Pretrial Detention: Lengthy pretrial detention was common. The large number of detainees, shortage of judges and court administrators, and judicial inefficiency resulted in trial delays.

e. Denial of Fair Public Trial

The provisional federal constitution states, "The judiciary is independent of the legislative and executive branches of government."

The civilian judicial system remained largely nonfunctional across the country. Some regions established local courts that depended on the dominant local clan and associated factions for their authority. The judiciary in most areas relied on some combination of traditional and customary law, sharia, and formal law. The judiciary was subject to influence and corruption. Authorities did not respect court orders. Civilian judges often feared trying cases, leaving military courts to try the majority of civilian cases.

In October 2014 Attorney General Ahmed Ali Dahir stated that more than 30 judges operating with unofficial documents had executed convictions, including death penalties. President Hassan Sheikh subsequently suspended 21 judges, stating the suspended judges "had been illegally in office." The attorney general stated the judgments made by the suspended judges would be re-examined, but results of the review were not made public by year's end.

In Somaliland functional courts existed, although there was a serious shortage of trained judges and legal documentation upon which to build judicial precedent. There was widespread interference in the judicial process, and government officials regularly intervened to influence cases, particularly those involving journalists. International NGOs reported local officials interfered in legal matters and invoked the public order law to detain and incarcerate persons without trial.

Puntland courts, while functional, lacked the capacity to provide equal protection under the law.

Traditional clan elders mediated conflicts throughout the country. Clans frequently used and applied traditional justice practices swiftly. Traditional judgments sometimes held entire clans or subclans responsible for alleged violations by individuals.

Under a pilot project funded by the United Nations beginning in 2008, mobile courts adjudicated 7,681 cases through September. These cases involved 497 clients across 25 districts in Somaliland. The mobile courts project in the southern and central regions suspended activities in 2013 for security reasons.

Trial Procedures

The provisional federal constitution states, "Every person has the right to a fair public hearing by an independent and impartial court or tribunal, to be held within a reasonable time." According to the provisional federal constitution, individuals have the right to be presumed innocent, to be informed promptly of the reason for their arrest or detention in a language they understand, to be brought before a competent court within 48 hours of arrest, to choose and consult with a legal practitioner, to be provided a legal practitioner by the state if they cannot afford one, and not to be compelled to incriminate themselves. The law extends these rights to all citizens, but authorities did not respect most rights relating to trial procedures. The provisional constitution does not address trial by jury, access to government-held evidence, confronting witnesses, the right to appeal a court's ruling, or the provision of sufficient time and facilities to prepare a defense.

Military courts tried civilians. Defendants in military courts rarely had legal representation or the right to appeal. Authorities sometimes executed those sentenced to death within days of the court's verdict (see section 1.a.). Some government officials continued to claim that a 2011 state of emergency decree gave military courts jurisdiction over crimes, including those committed by civilians, in parts of Mogadishu from which al-Shabaab had retreated. There was no clear government policy indicating whether this decree remained in effect.

In Somaliland defendants generally enjoyed a presumption of innocence and the right to a public trial, to be present at trial, and to consult an attorney at all stages of criminal proceedings. The government did not always inform defendants promptly and in detail of the charges against them and did not always provide access to government-held evidence. The government did not provide defendants with dedicated facilities to prepare a defense but generally provided adequate time to prepare. The government provided defendants with free interpretation or paid for private interpretation if they wished to decline government-offered interpretation. Defendants could question witnesses, present witnesses and evidence in their defense, and appeal court verdicts. Somaliland provided free legal representation for defendants who faced serious criminal charges and could not afford a private attorney. Defendants had the right not to be compelled to testify or confess guilt. A functioning legal aid clinic existed.

In Puntland clan elders resolved the majority of cases using customary law. The administration's more formalized judicial system addressed cases of those with no clan representation. Defendants generally enjoyed a presumption of innocence, the right to a public trial, and the right to be present and consult an attorney at all stages of criminal proceedings. Authorities did not always inform defendants promptly and in detail of the charges against them and did not always provide access to government-held evidence. Defendants had the right to present their own witnesses and evidence. Authorities did not provide defendants with dedicated facilities to prepare a defense but generally provided adequate time to prepare. Puntland authorities provided defendants with free interpretation services when needed. The government often delayed court proceedings for an unreasonable period.

There was no functioning formal judicial system in al-Shabaab-controlled areas. In sharia courts defendants generally did not defend themselves, present witnesses, or have an attorney represent them.

Political Prisoners and Detainees

The number of persons detained during the year for politically motivated reasons was unknown. Government and regional authorities arrested journalists as well as other persons critical of authorities (see section 2.a.).

Somaliland authorities allegedly kept Khatumo State supporters, arrested in 2014, in prison for political reasons. On September 22, forces belonging to the self-declared Khatumo State stormed a prison in Las-Anod, a town claimed by Somaliland in Sool Region, allegedly freeing approximately 20 political prisoners who supported Khatumo State. In remarks to the press, the vice president of Khatumo State, Abdalla Mohamed Ali, claimed Somaliland forces had abused these political prisoners.

Somaliland authorities continued to detain Somaliland residents employed by the federal government in Mogadishu, sometimes for extended periods. For example, on July 2, Somaliland forces arrested and detained Ahmed Hussein Sitin, a member of the federal parliament, for returning to Somaliland without government authorization.

Civil Judicial Procedures and Remedies

There were no known lawsuits seeking damages for, or cessation of, human rights violations in any region during the year, although the provisional federal constitution provides for "adequate procedures for redress of violations of human rights."

f. Arbitrary Interference with Privacy, Family, Home, or Correspondence

The provisional federal constitution states that "every person has the right to own, use, enjoy, sell, and transfer property" and that the private home is inviolable. Nonetheless, authorities searched property without warrants.

During the year AMISOM and Somali forces pushed al-Shabaab out of major towns and villages, including Taraka, Jungal, Duraned, Eel-elaan, Habakhaluul, Meyon, Magalay, Bardhere, Buur-dhuhunle, Kulun-jareer, Moragabey, Legaly, Gelewoyni, Ufurow, Eesow, Hasanow-Mumin, LIidaale, Makoon, Dhargo, and Manaas, forcing the organization to relinquish homes and land it had previously confiscated. The return of formerly displaced persons to these properties sometimes caused disputes over land ownership. There was no mechanism to address such disputes.

In Mogadishu the government and others evicted persons, mainly IDPs, from their homes without due process (see section 2.d.).

Government and regional authorities harassed relatives of al-Shabaab members.

On September 21, IJA security forces expelled 60 women allegedly married to al-Shabaab fighters from Kismayo, Lower Juba Region.

g. Use of Excessive Force and Other Abuses in Internal Conflicts

Killings: Conflict during the year involving the government, militias, AMISOM, and al-Shabaab resulted in the death and injury of civilians and the displacement of many others. Clan-based political violence in the Lower Shabelle and Middle Shabelle Regions involved revenge killings and attacks on civilian settlements. Clashes in the Hiraan, Galguduud, and Gedo Regions also resulted in deaths. Somaliland used military force to suppress supporters of the self-declared Khatumo State (see section 1.a.).

Conflict between Biimaal and Habar Gedir militias in the Lower Shabelle Region continued, although reports of abductions and killings decreased. Local civil society organizations continued to report that rape occurred in the context of fighting in Lower Shabelle. The ad hoc official commissions that the government established in 2014 to investigate alleged abuses by federal military forces and allied militias in the Lower Shabelle Region did not produce any reports.

Clashes throughout the south and central regions resulted in deaths and displacement. For example, on January 22, clashes between Dir and Hawadle clan militias over land in the towns of Burdhinle and Hada-Ogle in the Hiraan Region resulted in at least 23 deaths and numerous injuries.

Clan fighting revolving around the state formation process resulted in numerous deaths. ASWJ militias and federal forces skirmished throughout the year, causing internal displacement of persons. For example, on February 10, the ASWJ attacked SNA forces in Guri'el, Galguduud Region. According to local sources, fighting killed at least three civilians and injured many more.

Al-Shabaab continued to kill civilians. This included politically motivated killings that targeted civilians affiliated with the government and attacks on humanitarian NGO employees, UN staff, and diplomatic missions. Al-Shabaab often used suicide attacks, mortar attacks, and improvised explosive devices. It also killed prominent peace activists, community leaders, clan elders, and their family members for their roles in peace building, and it beheaded persons accused of spying for and collaborating with Somali national forces and affiliated militias.

There were numerous reported al-Shabaab attacks, including the February 20 vehicle-borne improvised explosive device attack on the Central Hotel in Mogadishu that killed approximately 25 persons, including government officials.

Fighting between al-Shabaab and AMISOM and Somali forces resulted in civilian deaths.

There were numerous reports that, on July 21, AMISOM Ugandan army troops killed at least 11 civilians, including a woman, two teenagers, and two elderly men, in separate incidents in the Jujuuma, Balle, and Rusiya neighborhoods of Merca, Lower Shabelle Region. Human Rights Watch also reported the alleged killing of six men on July 31 by AMISOM Ugandan army troops at a wedding in Merca.

<u>Abductions</u>: Al-Shabaab continued to abduct Somali civilians and foreign nationals; at year's end, several of them remained captive.

On July 9, Kenyan authorities announced the release of two Kenyan police officers abducted in Kenya and taken to Somalia by al-Shabaab in May 2013.

Al-Shabaab abducted humanitarian workers. In one case reported on April 13, al-Shabaab allegedly abducted three Somali national staff working for the NGO Solidarity between the towns of Garilley and Faafahdun, Gedo Region.

<u>Physical Abuse, Punishment, and Torture</u>: Government forces, allied militias, men wearing uniforms, and AMISOM troops committed sexual violence, including rape, of IDPs in and around Mogadishu. Al-Shabaab also committed sexual violence, including through forced marriages.

A September 2014 Human Rights Watch report documented 24 cases of sexual exploitation and abuse by Ugandan and Burundian AMISOM personnel. In five of the cases, the victims were under age 18. Cases included those in which girls and women reportedly were asked for sex in exchange for money, raped while seeking medical assistance or water, or raped and then given food or money. When releasing the results of its internal investigation on April 22, the chair of the African Union Commission, Nkosazana Dlamini-Zuma, qualified most of the allegations in the report as false and exaggerated, claiming only two of the 21 rape cases reported were potentially true. The report concluded that sex abuse by AMISOM troops did not appear to be widespread.

There were several casualties involving land mines and other unexploded ordnance. Landmine incidents were prevalent in the central region. For example, on September 22, two children died after ordnance they mistook as a toy exploded in Dom-Adi, Middle Shabelle Region.

<u>Child Soldiers</u>: During the year there were continued reports of the SNA and allied militia, the ASWJ, and al-Shabaab using child soldiers.

Implementation of the government's action plan with the United Nations to end the recruitment and use of children by the national army remained limited, although the federal government made additional progress.

In January, President Hassan Sheikh Mohamud signed a law ratifying the Convention on the Rights of the Child. Through the first eight months of the year, the SNA's Child Protection Unit (CPU) reported it conducted training awareness campaigns in Baidoa, Beledweyne, Kismayo, and Dinsoor on the importance of preventing child recruitment into the security forces. During screening missions with UN personnel, the CPU identified one child in the SNA's Jazeera training camp in March and 36 children at the Marina Camp in Kismayo in June. According to a global UN report on children in conflict, in 2014 a mobile SNA/UN team screened more than 1,000 soldiers and the Barre Aden Shire "Hirale" militia that surrendered in anticipation of integration into the national army. No children were found during the screening exercises.

The United Nations provided training on child protection to more than 8,000 SNA soldiers in collaboration with the EU Training Mission (EUTM) in Somalia and AMISOM. In addition, following UN advocacy, the AMISOM force commander issued a directive to reinforce accountability and compliance with children's rights during operations.

The United Nations supported the reintegration of 500 former child soldiers (375 boys, 125 girls) into their families and communities. Reintegration activities included the provision of psychosocial assistance, "back-to-school" support programs, and vocational training.

Authorities handed over children separated from armed groups to the UN Children's Fund (UNICEF).

Due to the absence of established birth registration systems, it was often difficult to determine the age of national security force recruits. The EUTM provided refresher training to approximately 500 Somali soldiers in Mogadishu, where they underwent interviews and screening to determine their ages. These screenings did not identify any children among the soldiers.

UN officials documented the recruitment and use of 819 children (779 boys, 40 girls) in 2014, including by al-Shabaab (437), the SNA and allied militia (197), Ahlu Sunna wal-Jama'a (109), and other armed elements (76). There were 133 children abducted: 97 by Al-Shabaab, 25 by the national army and allied militia, and 11 by unknown armed groups. More than half of the children al-Shabaab abducted were used to increase its numbers ahead of joint SNA/AMISOM operations.

Al-Shabaab continued to recruit and force children to participate in direct hostilities, including suicide attacks. Al-Shabaab raided schools, madrassas, and mosques for recruitment purposes. The United Nations reported 82 cases of child recruitment in mosques or during religious events convened by al-Shabaab. According to UN assessments, trends reflected in a 2012 Human Rights Watch report continued. These included children in al-Shabaab training camps subjected to grueling physical training, inadequate diet, weapons training, physical punishment, and religious training. The training also included forcing children to punish and execute other children. Al-Shabaab used children in combat, including placing them in front of other fighters to serve as human shields and suicide bombers. In August the CPU reported that 26 children who had previously served in al-Shabaab turned themselves in to federal government representatives in the Tieglow District. In addition, al-Shabaab used children in support roles, such as carrying ammunition, water, and food; removing injured and dead militants; gathering intelligence; and serving as guards. The organization sometimes used children to plant roadside bombs and other explosive devices. The Somali press frequently carried accounts of al-Shabaab indoctrinating children at schools and forcibly recruiting students into its ranks.

Other Conflict-related Abuses: Armed groups, particularly al-Shabaab, but also government forces and militia, deliberately restricted the passage of relief supplies and other items indispensable to the survival of the civilian population as well as access by humanitarian organizations, particularly in the southern and central regions.

Humanitarian workers regularly faced checkpoints, roadblocks, extortion, carjacking, and bureaucratic obstacles. Humanitarian organizations were often treated with suspicion and extorted. According to the United Nations, there were 15 reported incidents of denial of humanitarian access, the majority by unknown armed groups, and three each by al-Shabaab and the SNA.

There was small-scale diversion of World Food Program wet food commodities with suspected government involvement.

On January 22, the federal government arrested the mayor of Buulo-Burde, Osman Gedi Elmi, for mismanagement and diversion of food aid.

There were reports humanitarian access to the contested territories of Sool and Sanaag, between Somaliland and Puntland, was restricted. NGOs reported incidents of harassment by local authorities in both Somaliland and Puntland.

Al-Shabaab blocked critical transportation routes to prevent the delivery of humanitarian assistance to areas liberated by AMISOM in the southern and central regions. Human Rights Watch reported al-Shabaab imposed blockades around Hudur, Bulo-Burte, Elbur, Qoryoley, and other towns that had been liberated by AMISOM and Somali government forces, severely restricting the movement of goods, assistance, and persons.

Al-Shabaab restricted medical care, including restricting civilian travel to other areas for medical care, destroying medications provided by humanitarian agencies, and closing medical clinics.

International aid organizations evacuated their staff or halted food distribution and other aid-related activities in al-Shabaab-controlled areas due to killings, extortion, threats, harassment, expulsions, and prohibitions by al-Shabaab. International aid agencies increasingly relied on Somali staff and local organizations to deliver relief assistance in these areas.

Because of fighting between al-Shabaab, AMISOM, and the SNA, al-Shabaab's humanitarian access restrictions, taxation on livestock, failed water redistribution schemes, and insecurity, many residents in al-Shabaab-controlled areas fled to refugee camps in Kenya and Ethiopia and IDP camps in other areas of the country.

Section 2. Respect for Civil Liberties, Including:

a. Freedom of Speech and Press

The provisional federal constitution provides for freedom of speech and of the press. The federal government and regional authorities, however, subjected journalists to violence, harassment, arrest, and detention. Al-Shabaab killed five journalists, and harassed and threatened others.

For example, on July 26, al-Shabaab killed Abdihakin Mohamed Omar, a producer for Somali Broadcasting Corporation, and Mohamed Abdikarim Moallim Adam, a reporter for Universal TV in Gedo Region, during an attack on Jazeera Hotel in Mogadishu.

Freedom of Speech and Expression: Individuals in government-controlled areas were sometimes restricted from criticizing the government. Persons often lacked the ability to criticize authorities without reprisal, particularly to criticize officials' alleged corruption, their capacity to deal with security matters, and their mental and physical fitness to govern. In Somaliland Minister of Interior Ali Mohamed

Waranadde continued to harass opposition parties and pressured them not to engage in political discussions critical of the current administration. Waranadde also ordered hotels to deny opposition parties space to conduct political meetings.

According to Human Rights Watch, Somaliland authorities arrested human rights activist Guleid Ahmed Jama on April 18 after he made statements on the radio denouncing the executions of six persons convicted of murder by firing squad on April 13 and raising due process concerns. Authorities charged him with spreading "antinational" propaganda, initially held him in isolation, and denied him contact with his family; they released him on May 6.

Press and Media Freedoms: Print media consisted largely of short, photocopied independent daily newspapers, many of which the government owned, published in the larger cities. Several of these publications included criticism of political leaders and other prominent persons.

Most citizens obtained news from foreign radio broadcasts. According to the African Union, approximately 50 radio stations operated throughout the south and central regions as well as one shortwave station in Mogadishu. As in previous years, Somaliland authorities continued to prohibit the establishment of independent FM stations. All FM stations in Somaliland were government owned. There were at least six independent radio stations in Puntland.

Government and regional authorities temporarily closed media outlets.

For example, on January 3, NISA closed Radio Risaala and arrested director Mohamed Abdiwahab Abdullahi, chief editor Mohamed Kaafi Sheikh Abukarl, and a reporter, Mohamed Abdi, in Mogadishu for broadcasting reports about an alleged Ebola case. The three were released on January 8 without charge.

Between May and August, ASWJ militias temporarily closed down two radio stations and harassed and illegally detained journalists in Galgaduud Region. The militias imposed stern restrictions banning media organizations from reporting on the state formation process taking place in Adado, Galguduud Region, broadcasting news related to the federal government, relaying broadcasts of government-run Radio Mogadishu, and broadcasting news related to ASWJ without ASWJ's consent.

Somaliland authorities temporarily closed media organizations regularly, citing as reasons defamation or offending the president and other national leaders. For example, on January 12, the Hargeisa Court of Appeals ordered the closure of Haatuf newspaper in Hargeisa, one day after a regional court had lifted a ban on the publication. The newspaper was initially closed in April 2014 when Somaliland police stormed its offices for allegedly publishing false news.

On January 21, Puntland security forces arrested Hussein Yassin, editor of Shacabka Media, allegedly for criticizing the Puntland administration.

According to the Media Association of Puntland (MAP), on September 6, Puntland banned local radio stations from rebroadcasting programs or news generated by Mogadishu-based radio stations.

Violence and Harassment: The government, government-aligned militias, authorities in Somaliland and Puntland, ISWA, IGA, IJA, ASWJ, al-Shabaab, and unknown assailants abused and harassed journalists with impunity.

On January 4, NISA agents arbitrarily detained journalists Mohamed Salaad Osman and Ibrahim Haji Yusuf, who were covering an explosion in Mogadishu for Radio Goobjoog. The two were later released without charge.

On September 8, the MAP issued a press statement highlighting the alleged harassment and threats to the life of Voice of America (VOA) correspondent Faduma Yasin by the Bari Region police commissioner and governor following her September 6 report on the disappearance of an 18-month-old girl later found dead with her liver removed.

Journalists based in the Lower Juba Region continued to report that local security authorities harassed them.

According to the Somaliland Journalists Association, local authorities continued to systematically harass and arbitrarily detain journalists.

ASWJ militias arrested journalists in Dhusamareb, capital of the Interim Galmudug Administration. For example, on August 2 and 3, ASWJ forces detained the director of Dhusamareb-based Radio Codka Bartamaha, Nafiso Hersi Ogle, and two other employees for allegedly spreading false news. Journalist associations claimed the ASWJ abused these journalists while they were in detention.

Al-Shabaab and unknown persons continued to harass journalists. Journalists reported al-Shabaab threatened to kill them if they did not report positively on antigovernment attacks.

<u>Censorship or Content Restrictions</u>: Journalists engaged in rigorous self-censorship to avoid reprisals.

Al-Shabaab banned journalists from reporting news that undermined Islamic law as interpreted by al-Shabaab and forbade persons in areas under its control from listening to international media outlets.

<u>Libel/Slander Laws</u>: Puntland and Somaliland authorities also prosecuted journalists for libel.

<u>National Security</u>: Federal and regional authorities cited national security concerns to suppress criticism.

For example, on May 27, Puntland police arrested VOA reporter Faduma Yasin, a journalist working for the VOA-Somali service in Bosaso, for allegedly insulting Puntland president Abdiweli Gaas during an interview.

On July 6, Somaliland forces arrested prominent traditional leader Sultan Mohamed Muse Cune after the sultan responded to a statement by Interior Minister Waranaade threatening to arrest anyone who protested against the president by stating that Waranaade was a spy of former Somali dictator Siyad Barre. In a press conference, the governor of Togdheer Region, Mohamed Muse Diiriye, vowed to take the sultan to court.

Internet Freedom

Authorities did not restrict access to the internet, and there were no credible reports that the government monitored private online communications without appropriate legal authority. Al-Shabaab prohibited companies from providing access to the internet and forced telecommunication companies to shut down data services in al-Shabaab-controlled areas.

According to the International Telecommunication Union, 1.63 percent of the population used the internet in 2014.

Academic Freedom and Cultural Events

Academics practiced self-censorship. The Puntland administration required individuals to obtain government permits to conduct academic research.

Except in al-Shabaab-controlled areas, there were no official restrictions on attending cultural events, playing music, or going to the cinema. The security situation, however, effectively restricted access to and organization of cultural events in the southern and central regions.

b. Freedom of Peaceful Assembly and Association

Freedom of Assembly

The federal provisional constitution provides for freedom of assembly, although in practice this right was limited. A general lack of security effectively limited this right in many areas.

Regional authorities allegedly killed protesters (also see section 1.a.).

For example, on February 2, Somaliland forces beat protesters gathering to complain about a recent border closure in Lowyado town, Awdal Region, between Somaliland and Djibouti. Local media reported one protester later died from injuries sustained during the event.

The federal Ministry of Interior continued to require its approval for all public gatherings, citing security concerns such as the risk of attack by al-Shabaab suicide bombers.

The Somaliland government banned political parties from holding meetings in hotels or public arenas in an effort to suppress opposition to the government.

Al-Shabaab did not allow any gatherings without its prior consent.

Freedom of Association

The provisional federal constitution provides for freedom of association. NGOs reportedly faced harassment by government officials. There were also reports that regional authorities restricted freedom of association.

Persons in the southern and central regions outside of al-Shabaab-controlled areas could freely join civil society organizations focusing on a wide range of problems. Al-Shabaab did not allow most international NGOs to operate. Citizens generally respected civil society organizations for their ability to deliver social services in the absence of functioning government ministries.

Regional administrations took steps to control or gain benefit from humanitarian organizations, including by imposing registration requirements; attempting to control humanitarian contracting, procurement, and staffing; and collecting fees.

Some Puntland civil society members alleged interference by security forces in activities during the year.

Somaliland authorities prevented civil society from participating in meetings related to the federal process, which it perceived as undermining Somaliland independence claims.

c. Freedom of Religion

See the Department of State's *International Religious Freedom Report* at www.state.gov/religiousfreedomreport/.

d. Freedom of Movement, Internally Displaced Persons, Protection of Refugees, and Stateless Persons

The provisional federal constitution states that all persons lawfully residing within the country have the right to freedom of movement, to choose their residence, and to leave the country. Freedom of movement, however, was restricted in some parts of the country.

The government and Somaliland authorities cooperated with the Office of the UN High Commissioner for Refugees (UNHCR) and the International Organization for Migration (IOM) on assistance to IDPs, refugees, returning refugees, asylum seekers, stateless persons, and other persons of concern.

In-country Movement: Checkpoints operated by government forces, allied groups, armed militias, clan factions, and al-Shabaab (see section 1.g.) inhibited movement and exposed citizens to looting, extortion, harassment, and violence. For example, on March 3, fighting between SNA and NISA forces over control of a roadblock near Afgoye town, Lower Shabelle Region, allegedly resulted in several fatalities and many injured.

Somaliland prohibited federal officials, including those of Somaliland origin, from entering Somaliland. It also prevented its citizens from traveling to Mogadishu to participate in federal government processes or in cultural activities. On September 27, for example, Somaliland security forces arrested four Somaliland musicians upon their arrival at Egal airport in the Somaliland capital of Hargeisa for having travelled to Mogadishu to perform during the Eid al-Adha celebrations.

Galmudug officials denied entry to Puntland residents. In an announcement on January 26, then Galmudug traffic supervisor Mohamud Mohamed Abdulle stated the Galmudug administration would fine vehicles bearing Puntland license plates and arrest the driver for 24 hours.

Puntland authorities allegedly continued to ban the transport of relief items by road from the port of Berbera in Somaliland to towns in Puntland, including Garowe and Galkayo. The ban limited the ability of aid workers to deliver humanitarian supplies, such as food, livestock vaccination equipment, nutritional supplements, and education supplies, to vulnerable populations in Puntland.

Foreign Travel: Few citizens had the means to obtain passports. In view of widespread passport fraud, many foreign governments did not recognize Somali passports as valid travel documents.

Internally Displaced Persons (IDPs)

Conflict, including fighting between clan militias in the Lower Shabelle, Middle Shabelle, and Hiraan regions, and drought resulted in continued displacement and new displacements. There were more than 1.1 million IDPs across the country, mainly in the southern and central regions. Of the total, 369,000 persons were located in Mogadishu. According to UNHCR, renewed AMISOM and security force offensives against al-Shabaab caused most new displacements. UNHCR estimated at least 42,000 persons had fled areas in south-central Somalia where offensives had taken place.

Saudi Arabia continued to repatriate Somalis forcibly. From December 2013 to September, the country received an estimated 70,000 forced returnees from Saudi Arabia. The IOM assisted approximately 15,000 of these persons, providing many with onward transportation by road and air. Many of these forced returnees became IDPs in the country upon their return, since they were unable to return to their places of origin. Forced deportations from Saudi Arabia continued through the end of the year.

Somalis and citizens from other countries fleeing the conflict in Yemen sought refuge in Somalia. By September approximately 30,000 individuals had arrived in the country, of whom 90 percent were Somali citizens. UNHCR provided returnees with temporary lodging and financial assistance. By September the IOM also provided 8,020 returnees with onward transportation assistance. Most Somali returnees returned to locations in south-central Somalia, with 55 percent travelling to Mogadishu. On several occasions the Somaliland government threatened to close the port and prohibit the disembarkation of Somalis not originally from Somaliland.

UNHCR continued to assist IDPs. The United Nations sought a commitment from the government to address returnees, evictions, and related humanitarian problems in Mogadishu. Government and regional authorities provided negligible protection and assistance to IDPs; the response in government areas was largely ineffective because of limited resources and capacity and poor coordination. Private persons with claims to land and government authorities regularly pursued the forceful eviction of IDPs in Mogadishu.

Somali authorities did not prevent the forced displacement of persons from shelters to camps on the outskirts of the city. Some IDPs and humanitarian agencies criticized local authorities for tacitly endorsing the forceful relocation of IDPs to insecure areas in Mogadishu.

In the first half of the year, almost 100,000 persons, the vast majority of them IDPs, were forcibly evicted from Mogadishu and other urban areas in the Juba, South West, and Puntland Regions. Insecure land tenure and limited land title verification contributed to the large scale of forced evictions.

According to UNHCR, 10,647 households (approximately 65,000 persons) were evicted in Mogadishu from January to August. Of that number, many were IDPs and most were forcibly evicted. In almost all cases, the individuals concerned were only notified orally of their pending eviction. IDPs and others evicted were forced to leave public land that was claimed by individuals. Such evictions continued during the year.

An April 20 Human Rights Watch report alleged that Somali national police, NISA forces, and city council police forcibly evicted an estimated 21,000 displaced persons in Mogadishu during March. The report claimed Somali authorities beat some of the evicted, destroyed their shelters, and left them without water, food, or other assistance. According to the report, authorities failed to provide adequate notification and compensation to the communities facing eviction and did not provide viable relocation or local integration options as required by international law. The report claimed that none of the evicted persons interviewed for the report had seen an official written eviction order and that most were unaware of the planned evictions.

Government forces and aligned militia looted and collaborated in the diversion of humanitarian aid from intended beneficiaries in Mogadishu. Most international aid organizations previously evacuated their staff or halted food distribution and other aid-related activities in al-Shabaab-controlled areas due to continued killings, extortion, threats, and harassment.

Government forces, allied militias, men wearing uniforms, and AMISOM troops committed sexual violence, including rape of IDPs in and around Mogadishu. Many of the victims were children. Women and children living in IDP settlements in Bosaaso, Galkayo, Hargeisa, and along the Afgoye corridor continued to report a large number of rapes.

Gatekeepers in control of some IDP camps reportedly forced girls and women to provide sex acts in exchange for food and services within the camps.

On January 19, a 13-year-old girl reported being raped by two Somali soldiers near her home at the Ex-Control IDP camp in Mogadishu when fetching water on her own. According to the local press, after the victim's mother complained to local authorities with the help of village elders, local police paid the family "$300 in compensation for breaking the girl's virginity and $200 for humiliating her dignity." The victim's mother lamented that the two rapists remained at large, and she continued to see them every day "wielding their AK-47 rifles on the street."

Protection of Refugees

Access to Asylum: The provisional federal constitution states that every person who has sought refuge in the country has the right not to be returned or taken to any country in which that person has a well-founded fear of persecution. There was no official system for providing such protection, however. Somaliland continued to register asylum seekers with the assistance of UNHCR. From July the Somaliland Ministry of Rehabilitation, Resettlement, and Reconstruction registered approximately 800 new arrivals and asylum seekers. In some instances, the Somaliland government refused to register Ethiopians and Eritreans as asylum seekers. UNHCR reported that 5,800 refugees and 9,720 registered asylum seekers resided in the country; most came from the Oromiya and Ogaden regions of Ethiopia and Yemen.

Refugee Abuse: Refugees lacked sufficient access to protection through law enforcement and the justice system.

Section 3. Freedom to Participate in the Political Process

In 2012 the TFG completed the 2011 *Roadmap for Ending the Transition*, collaborating with representatives of Puntland, Galmudug, the ASWJ, and the international community. The process included drafting a provisional federal constitution, forming an 825-member National Constituent Assembly (NCA) that ratified the provisional constitution, having elders select a 275-member federal parliament, and holding speakership and presidential elections. The provisional constitution provides citizens the ability to choose their government in free and fair periodic elections based on universal and equal suffrage, but citizens could not exercise that ability. The federal parliament had not passed election-related laws by year's end.

Elections and Political Participation

Recent Elections: In May 2012 under the roadmap process, 135 traditional clan elders convened in Mogadishu to nominate 825 NCA delegates to consider the provisional federal constitution. The elders also nominated candidates for the country's 275-member federal parliament to serve four-year terms under the provisional constitution. There were accusations of bribery and intimidation involved in the selection of the 135 traditional elders and in their nomination of parliamentarians, but overall the roadmap signatories and others viewed parliamentarians as broadly representative of their communities.

A 27-member technical selection committee, assisted by international observers from the African Union, the League of Arab States, the EU, the Intergovernmental Authority on Development, the Organization of Islamic Cooperation, and the UN Political Office for Somalia, vetted and approved the delegates and federal parliament nominees submitted by the traditional elders. In some cases, committee members and their families received threats and intimidation during the process. In August 2012 the NCA ratified the provisional federal constitution. The inauguration of the federal parliament occurred the same month. The parliament subsequently elected Mohamed Sheikh Osman "Jawari" as its speaker.

In September 2012, in the presence of international observers, the parliament held an indirect presidential election through a secret ballot in which Hassan Sheikh Mohamud defeated incumbent TFG president Sheikh Sharif in the second and final round of voting. There were unsubstantiated reports of presidential candidates' bribing parliamentarians in exchange for their vote. Sheikh Sharif conceded defeat and described the vote as fair.

In December 2013 the parliament passed a no-confidence measure against Prime Minister Abdi Farah Shirdon and subsequently approved Abdiweli Sheikh Ahmed as the new prime minister. He expanded the Council of Ministers (cabinet) from 10 ministers to 25. In October 2014 Prime Minister Abdiweli announced a cabinet reshuffle; however, the president objected, and ministers remained in the same positions. In December 2014 the parliament passed a no-confidence measure against Prime Minister Abdiweli, and the president subsequently appointed Omar Abdirashid Ali Sharmarke to serve as the new prime minister. The parliament approved Sharmarke's appointment in December 2014. Prime Minister Sharmarke appointed his new cabinet on February 9. On June 29, President Mohamud announced that the country would not conduct one-person, one-vote elections in 2016. On September 21, the federal government launched the National Consultative Forum, which tasked federal and regional government representatives and civil society with defining an electoral process for 2016.

Somaliland laws prevent citizens in its region from participating in the federal government-related processes.

Puntland has a single-chamber, 66-member House of Representatives; a council of elders selected its members in 2008. In 2009 the council selected Abdirahman Mohamed Mohamud "Farole" as president. In 2012 Puntland's constituent assembly overwhelmingly adopted a state constitution that enshrines a multiparty political system. The constitution's adoption also extended the four-year term for which "Farole" was selected by one year, to January 2014, since the constitution called for a five-year presidential term moving forward. In January 2014 Abdiweli Mohamed Ali defeated incumbent President Farole by one parliamentary vote in a run-off election broadcast live on local television and radio stations. President Farole accepted the results. The parliament also elected Abdihakim Abdulahi as the new vice president.

In January 2014 the Puntland Ministry of Constitution, Federal Affairs, and Democratization was established by presidential decree. The new ministry was tasked with conducting a constitutional review process for Puntland, implementing federal *Vision 2016* objectives (state formation, elections, and review of the federal constitution), and advancing the democratization process in Puntland.

In June 2014 two contesting state formation conferences, the South West Six and South West Three, signed an agreement in Mogadishu to merge, reconcile, and launch a single Interim South West Administration (ISWA) composed of the Somali regions of Bay, Bakool, and Lower Shabelle. In November 2014, 373 of 396 total conference delegates voted to elect Sharif Hassan Sheikh Adan as ISWA's first president, thus officially establishing the interim administration. The ISWA had not formed its local assembly by year's end.

On June 22, the federal government officially inaugurated the 89-member Interim Galmudug Administration (IGA) Assembly. Forty traditional elders representing 11 subclans selected the 89-member assembly. On July 4, 50 members of the 89-member assembly elected Abdikarim Hussein Guled as the IGA's first president. ASWJ refused to accept the election results and unilaterally established its own self-declared administration for the central regions.

In Somaliland, parliamentary elections, last held in 2005, were overdue. Somaliland president Ahmed Mohamed Mohamud "Silanyo" was elected in 2010. International and domestic observers declared the election free and fair. Somaliland has a bicameral parliament consisting of an appointed 82-member House of Elders, known as the Guurti, and an elected 82-member House of Representatives with proportional clan representation. In April the House of Elders voted to postpone the delayed election for the House of Representatives and president until March 2017. There were allegations the House of Elders was subject to political corruption and undue influence.

On August 18, the Somaliland Constitutional Court ruled to uphold the House of Elders' decision to delay parliamentary and presidential elections until March 2017. The Constitutional Court also set the election of the House of Elders for March 2018.

In May 2013 approximately 500 elders and representatives from the regions of Lower Juba, Upper Juba, and Gedo convened to elect leaders for the then unrecognized "Jubaland state." They selected the leader of the Ras Kamboni militia, Ahmed Mohamed Islam "Madobe," as president. Clans opposed to him organized militias. Violent clashes ensued, causing civilian displacement and reportedly more than 80 civilian casualties. In August 2013 the federal government and Jubaland delegates signed an agreement that resulted in the federal government's formal recognition of the newly formed Interim Juba Administration (IJA). Before the conclusion of its two-year interim mandate, on April 15, President Madobe inaugurated the 75-member IJA assembly. The assembly selected him to be president on August 15.

Al-Shabaab prohibited citizens in the areas it controlled from changing their al-Shabaab administrators. Some al-Shabaab administrations, however, consulted local traditional elders on specific issues and allowed preexisting district committees to remain in place.

Political Parties and Political Participation: There were no official political parties in the southern and central regions, and there was no mechanism to register parties. Several political associations, however, described themselves as parties. For example, President Hassan Sheikh claimed to be elected from the Peace and Development Party. The provisional constitution provides that every citizen has the right to take part in public affairs and that this right includes forming political parties, participating in their activities, and being elected for any position within a political party. On July 6, the parliament approved the nine members of the National Independent Electoral Commission. The commission did not regulate the political party system, and its role in facilitating a political transition during the year remained unclear. The Somaliland and Puntland constitutions and electoral legislation limit the number of political parties to three and establish conditions pertaining to their political programs, finances, and constitutions.

Participation of Women and Minorities: The roadmap signatories agreed that, prior to the transition to a permanent government, the federal parliament should consist of at least 30 percent women, but women held only 14 percent of 275 seats in parliament. The government's 26-member cabinet had three female members. Cultural/traditional practices that prevented women from participating fully in political life included the popular notions that women should stay at home, the lack of legitimacy given to women in politics by traditional elders, and women's own reluctance to participate in the political process.

Civil society, minority clans, and Puntland authorities called for the abolition of the "4.5 formula" by which political representation was divided among the four major clans, with the minority clans combined as the remaining "0.5" share. This system allocated minority clans a fixed and low number of slots in the federal parliament. The roadmap signatories agreed to the system prior to the transition to a permanent government. According to the agreement, the system was not to carry over into the 2016 parliamentary elections.

Former prime minister Shirdon and President Hassan Sheikh broke with the 4.5-clan allocation formula in their 2012 appointment of two minority clan members to the 10-member cabinet. Former prime minister Abdiweli and Prime Minister Sharmarke maintained the same ratio of minority representation when expanding the cabinet.

Somaliland had two women in its 86-member House of Representatives. The sole woman occupying a seat in the House of Elders gained appointment after her husband, who occupied the seat, resigned in 2012. Women traditionally were excluded from the House of Elders. There was one female minister among the 24 cabinet ministers. The Somaliland cabinet included no minorities.

A woman chaired the Somaliland Human Rights Commission, while a minority youth served as deputy chair. The Somaliland president kept a presidential advisor on minority problems.

Women have never served on the Council of Elders in Puntland. Traditional clan elders, all men, selected members of Puntland's House of Representatives. Two women served in the 66-member House of Representatives. The minister of women and family affairs and the minster of constitution, federalism, and democratization were women. The nine-member electoral commission included one woman.

Section 4. Corruption and Lack of Transparency in Government

Government officials frequently engaged in corrupt practices. The law provides for criminal penalties for corruption by officials. The government did not implement the law effectively.

Corruption: The provisional constitution called for establishment of an independent anticorruption commission in 2012 with a mandate to investigate allegations of corruption in the public sector. The federal government established the commission in January, but no cases were brought to the body by year's end.

The October 2014 report by the UN Monitoring Group on Somalia and Eritrea (SEMG) indicated corruption continued as did "patterns of misappropriation with diversion rates between 70 and 80 percent." The report also addressed "secret contracting," in which officials signed contracts regarding public assets without transparency or oversight. It stated "individuals close to the presidency" were working to gain control of recovered overseas assets that should have gone to the central bank. The report stated the central bank made payments to private persons or office holders for private purposes and reported on diversion of revenue from Mogadishu's port. Allegations persisted that diversion of government revenue for private purposes continued unabated.

A 2015 SEMG annex report documented that the Soma Oil and Gas company paid more than half a million dollars to senior civil servants in the Ministry of Petroleum and Mineral Resources under the rubric of "capacity building agreement." The report detailed several ministry officials receiving salaries simultaneously from the federal government and Soma Oil and Gas Company. The international oil production sharing agreement between Soma Oil and the federal government gave the company extremely favorable terms.

The Financial Governance Committee (FGC) consisted of three members of international financial institutions and three members of the federal government. The body reviewed 13 contracts during the year. Of the contracts reviewed, four were never approved or implemented and two were adjusted in line with FGC recommendations. The FGC did not receive a substantive federal government response on seven contracts it reviewed.

The FGS appointed an accountant general in July. Neither he nor the auditor general had publicly released any reports by years' end.

The SEMG continued to report on the export of charcoal in violation of a UN Security Council ban. The report discussed charcoal production in areas controlled by al-Shabaab, the IJA, and Kenyan AMISOM forces as well as its export, which the SEMG reported to be primarily from Kismayo. Internationally registered vessels fished illegally in the country's territorial waters. Officials stated such illegal practices represented millions of dollars of forgone income for the government.

Somaliland had a national auditor and a governance and anticorruption commission appointed by Somaliland's president. Somaliland did not try any Somaliland officials for corruption.

Puntland's Good Governance and Anticorruption Commission did not try any Puntland officials for corruption.

Al-Shabaab extorted high and unpredictable "zakat" (a Muslim obligation to donate to charity during Ramadan) and "sadaqa" (a voluntary charity contribution paid by Muslims) taxes in the regions it controlled. It also diverted and stole humanitarian food aid.

Financial Disclosure: The law does not require income and asset disclosure by appointed or elected officials.

Public Access to Information: The provisional constitution states that citizens have the right of access to information held by the state. It also states that parliament shall enact a law to provide for this right, but parliament had not approved such a law by year's end.

Section 5. Governmental Attitude Regarding International and Nongovernmental Investigation of Alleged Violations of Human Rights

A number of local and international human rights groups operated in areas outside al-Shabaab-controlled territory, investigating and publishing their findings on human rights cases. Government officials were somewhat cooperative and responsive to their views, although they also harassed NGOs. Security concerns constrained NGOs' ability to operate in southern and central areas. International and local NGOs generally worked without major restrictions in Puntland and Somaliland.

Authorities sometimes harassed or did not cooperate with NGOs. For example, in matters related to official corruption, the government regularly dismissed the findings of international and local NGOs as well as of internal auditors.

Government Human Rights Bodies: The provisional federal constitution calls for an independent national human rights commission and a truth and reconciliation commission to be formed within 45 days and 30 days, respectively, of the formation of the Council of Ministers in 2012. These commissions had not been formed by year's end.

Limited resources as well as inexperienced commissioners restricted the effectiveness of the Somaliland Human Rights Commission and Puntland's Human Rights Defender Office.

Section 6. Discrimination, Societal Abuses, and Trafficking in Persons

The provisional federal constitution states that all citizens, regardless of sex, religion, social or economic status, political opinion, clan, disability, occupation, birth, dialect, age, race, color, tribe, ethnicity, culture, or wealth, shall have equal rights and duties before the law. The constitution and law do not prohibit discrimination based on national origin or citizenship, social origin, HIV status, or having other communicable diseases. The provisional constitution does not prohibit discrimination based on sexual orientation or gender identity. Authorities did not enforce antidiscrimination provisions effectively in any of the regions.

Women

Rape and Domestic Violence: The law criminalizes rape, providing penalties of five to 15 years in prison for violations. Sentences from military courts for rape included death. The government did not effectively enforce the law. There are no laws against spousal violence, including rape. Somali NGOs documented patterns of rape perpetrated with impunity, particularly of displaced women (see section 2.d.) and members of minority clans.

Although statistics on cases of gender-based violence in Mogadishu were unreliable, international and local NGOs characterized such violence as pervasive. Government forces, militia members, and men wearing uniforms raped women and girls. While the army arrested some security force members accused of such rapes, impunity was the norm. AMISOM troops committed sexual abuse and exploitation, including rape (see section 1.g.).

Local civil society organizations reported several cases of gang rape. For example, in May a 14-year-old girl was allegedly gang-raped after attackers forced her off a minibus taxi. After the case was reported to a Criminal Investigation Department station, the police officer in charge refused to file the complaint and instead detained the victim for making false claims. The victim claimed the police officer that ordered her arrest repeatedly raped her.

According to local human rights organizations, IGA security forces in Galinsoor (between Galkaayo and Adaado) gang-raped four women on August 29. The incident was brought to the attention of IGA authorities, but no legal action was taken against the perpetrators.

Women feared reporting rape due to possible reprisals. Police were reluctant to investigate and sometimes asked survivors to do the investigatory work for their own cases. Traditional approaches to dealing with rape tended to ignore the survivor's situation and instead sought resolution or compensation for rape through a negotiation between members of the perpetrator's and survivor's clans. Some survivors were forced to marry perpetrators.

For the most part, authorities rarely used formal structures to address rape. Survivors suffered from subsequent discrimination based on the attribution of "impurity."

Al-Shabaab sentenced persons to death for rape.

Local civil society organizations in Somaliland reported that gang rape continued to be a problem in urban areas, primarily perpetrated by youth gangs and male students. It often occurred in poorer neighborhoods and among immigrants, returned refugees, and displaced rural populations living in urban areas. According to 2013 data from a local Hargeisa-based NGO, gang rapes constituted 30 percent of reported rapes. In 55 percent of reported cases, a minor was the victim. Many cases went unreported.

Domestic and sexual violence against women remained serious problems despite the provisional federal constitution provision prohibiting any form of violence against women. While both sharia and customary law address the resolution of family disputes, women were not included in the decision-making process.

Female Genital Mutilation/Cutting: Although the provisional federal constitution describes female circumcision as cruel and degrading, equates it with torture, and prohibits the circumcision of girls, FGM/C is almost universally practiced throughout the country. UNICEF reported that 98 percent of women and girls had undergone FGM/C and that the majority were subjected to infibulation--the most severe form--which involves cutting and sewing the genitalia. At least 80 percent of Somali girls who have undergone FGM/C had the procedure performed when they were between the ages of five and 14. International and local NGOs conducted education awareness programs on the dangers of FGM/C, but there were no reliable statistics to measure their success.

Other Harmful Traditional Practices: Al-Shabaab killed women in the areas it controlled. For example, on September 28, al-Shabaab publicly stoned a woman to death in Barawe, Lower Shabelle Region, after declaring her guilty of adultery.

Sexual Harassment: The provisional federal constitution states that all workers, particularly women, shall have a special right of protection from sexual abuse and discrimination. There were no data on, laws pertaining to, or governmental programs addressing sexual harassment, although it was believed to be widespread in all regions.

Reproductive Rights: A woman's husband often made decisions regarding the couple's reproduction. Women had very limited ability to decide freely and responsibly the number, spacing, and timing of their children or manage their reproductive health. Very limited information about and little access to contraception was available to women. According to the United Nations, an estimated 1.5 percent of girls and women between the ages of 15 and 49 had access to a modern method of contraception. Women rarely had skilled attendants during pregnancy and childbirth, emergency care for complications arising from abortion, or essential obstetric and postpartum care.

The United Nations reported that more than 80 percent of internally displaced women had no access to safe maternal delivery. The maternal mortality ratio was 850 per 100,000 live births due to complications during labor that often involved anemia, FGM/C, and the lack of medical care. A woman's lifetime risk of maternal death was one in 18.

Discrimination: Women did not have the same rights as men and experienced systematic subordination to men, despite provisions in the federal constitution prohibiting such discrimination. Women experienced discrimination in credit, education, and housing.

Only men administered sharia, which was often applied in the interests of men. According to sharia and the local tradition of blood compensation, anyone found guilty of the death of a woman paid to the victim's family only half the amount required to compensate for a man's death.

The law requires equal pay for equal work. Women formed a negligible part of those employed in both the formal public and private sectors because of girls' low education level. Women were not subject to discrimination in owning or managing businesses, except in al-Shabaab-controlled areas. Al-Shabaab claimed women's participation in economic activities was anti-Islamic.

While formal law and sharia provide women the right to own and dispose of property independently, various legal, cultural, and societal barriers often obstructed women from exercising such rights. By law girls and women could inherit only half the amount of property to which their brothers were entitled. A 2010 report from a local women's organization in Somaliland indicated 75 percent of women did not own livestock, land, or other property. Only 15 to 20 percent received inheritance from male family members.

Children

Birth Registration: The provisional federal constitution provides that there is only one Somali citizenship and calls for a special law defining how to obtain, suspend, or lose it. As of year's end, parliament had not passed such a law.

According to 2005-12 UNICEF data, authorities registered 3 percent of births in the country. Authorities in Puntland and in the southern and central regions did not register births. Birth registration occurred in Somaliland for hospital and home births, but limited capacity combined with the nomadic lifestyle of many persons caused numerous births in the region to go unregistered. In November 2014 UNICEF began to support the Somaliland government in establishing a birth registration system in two districts. During the year UNICEF helped expand the system to six districts. Failure to register births did not result in denial of public services, such as education.

Education: The provisional constitution provides the right to a free education up to the secondary level, but education was neither tuition-free, compulsory, nor universal. Education needs were partially met by a patchwork of institutions, including a traditional system of Quranic schools; public primary and secondary school systems financed by communities, foreign donors, and the Somaliland and Puntland administrations; Islamic charity-run schools; and a number of privately run primary and secondary schools and vocational training institutes. In many areas children did not have access to schools other than madrassas. Attendance rates for girls remained lower than for boys.

Child Abuse: Child abuse and rape of children were serious problems, although no statistics on their prevalence were available. There were no known efforts by the government or regional governments to combat child abuse. Children remained among the chief victims of continuing societal violence.

The practice of "asi walid," a custom whereby parents placed their children in boarding schools, other institutions, and sometimes prison for disciplinary purposes and without any legal procedure, allegedly continued throughout the country.

Early and Forced Marriage: The provisional federal constitution does not specify a minimum legal age for marriage. It notes marriage requires the free consent of both the man and woman to be legal. Early marriages frequently occurred; 45 percent of women between the ages of 20 and 24 were married by age 18, and 8 percent were married by age 15. In rural areas parents often compelled daughters as young as 12 to marry. In areas under its control, al-Shabaab arranged compulsory marriages between its soldiers and young girls and used the lure of marriage as a recruitment tool. There were no known efforts by the government or regional authorities to prevent early and forced marriage.

Female Genital Mutilation/Cutting: See information on girls under 18 in the women's section above.

Sexual Exploitation of Children: Child prostitution is illegal in all regions. There is no statutory rape law or minimum age for consensual sex. The law does not expressly prohibit child pornography. The law on sexual exploitation was rarely enforced, and such exploitation reportedly was frequent.

Child Soldiers: The use of child soldiers remained a problem (see section 1.g.).

Displaced Children: There was a large population of IDPs and children who lived and worked on the streets (see section 2.d.).

International Child Abductions: The country is not a party to the 1980 Hague Convention on the Civil Aspects of International Child Abduction. For information see the Department of State's report on compliance at travel.state.gov/content/childabduction/en/legal/compliance.html.

Anti-Semitism

There was no known Jewish community, and there were no reports of anti-Semitic acts.

Trafficking in Persons

See the Department of State's Trafficking in Persons Report at www.state.gov/j/tip/rls/tiprpt/.

Persons with Disabilities

The provisional federal constitution provides equal rights before the law for persons with disabilities and prohibits the state from discriminating against them. Authorities did not enforce these provisions. The provisional federal constitution does not specify whether this provision applies to physical, intellectual, mental, or sensory disabilities. It does not discuss discrimination by nongovernmental actors, including with regard to employment, education, air travel and other transportation, or provision of health care. The law does not mandate access to buildings, information, or communications for persons with disabilities.

The needs of most persons with disabilities were not addressed. A report by the World Health Organization and Swedish International Development Aid (SIDA estimated up to 15 percent of the population was physically disabled. In 2011 SIDA found that 25 percent of public buildings were designed to make them accessible for wheelchair users but that there were no public transportation facilities with wheelchair access.

In a March report, Amnesty International stated that persons with disabilities faced daily human rights abuses, such as unlawful killings, violence including rape and other forms of sexual violence, forced evictions, and lack of access to health care or an adequate standard of living. The report described domestic violence and forced marriage as prevalent practices affecting persons with disabilities. It added that women and girls with disabilities faced an increased risk of rape and other forms of sexual violence, often with impunity, due to perceptions their disabilities were a burden to the family or that such persons were of less value and could therefore be abused.

Several local NGOs in Somaliland provided services for persons with disabilities and reported numerous cases of discrimination and abuse. These NGOs reported that persons with mental and physical disabilities faced widespread discrimination and that it was common and condoned by the community for students without disabilities to beat and harass students with disabilities.

Without a public health infrastructure, few services existed to provide support or education for persons with mental disabilities. It was common for such persons to be chained to a tree or restrained within their homes.

Local organizations advocated for the rights of persons with disabilities with negligible support from local authorities.

National/Racial/Ethnic Minorities

More than 85 percent of the population shared a common ethnic heritage, religion, and nomad-influenced culture. In most areas the predominant clan excluded members of other groups from effective participation in governing institutions and subjected them to discrimination in employment, judicial proceedings, and access to public services.

Minority groups included the Bantu (the largest minority group), Benadiri, Rer Hamar, Brawanese, Swahili, Tumal, Yibir, Yaxar, Madhiban, Hawrarsame, Muse Dheryo, Faqayaqub, and Gabooye. Custom restricted intermarriage between minority groups and mainstream clans. Minority groups, often lacking armed militias, continued to be disproportionately subjected to killings, torture, rape, kidnapping for ransom, and looting of land and property with impunity by faction militias and majority clan members, often with the acquiescence of federal and local authorities. Many minority communities continued to live in deep poverty and to suffer from numerous forms of discrimination and exclusion.

Representatives of minority clans in the federal parliament were targeted by unknown assailants, whom minority clan members alleged were paid by majority clan members. For example, on July 25, unidentified gunmen assassinated minority parliamentarian Abdullahi Hussein Muse Bantu in a drive-by shooting in Mogadishu.

Acts of Violence, Discrimination, and Other Abuses Based on Sexual Orientation and Gender Identity

Same-sex sexual contact is punishable by imprisonment for two months to three years. The law does not prohibit discrimination based on sexual orientation or gender identity. Society considered sexual orientation and gender identity taboo topics, and there was no known public discussion of discrimination based on sexual orientation or gender identity in any region. There were no known LGBTI organizations and no reports of events. There were few reports of societal violence or discrimination based on sexual orientation or gender identity due to severe societal stigma that prevented LGBTI individuals from making their sexual orientation or gender identity known publicly. There were no known actions to investigate or punish those complicit in abuses. Hate crime laws or other criminal justice mechanisms did not exist to aid in the prosecution of bias-motivated crimes against members of the LGBTI community.

HIV and AIDS Social Stigma

Persons with HIV/AIDS continued to face discrimination and abuse in their local communities and by employers in all regions. The United Nations reported that persons with HIV/AIDS experienced physical abuse, rejection by their families, and workplace discrimination and dismissal. Children with HIV-positive parents also suffered discrimination, which hindered access to services. There was no official response to such discrimination.

Section 7. Worker Rights

a. Freedom of Association and the Right to Collective Bargaining

The provisional federal constitution provides for the right of every worker to form and join a trade union, to participate in the activities of a trade union, to conduct legal strikes, and to engage in collective bargaining. No specific legal restrictions existed that limited these rights. The law does not provide limits on the scope of collective bargaining. The provisional federal constitution does not address antiunion discrimination or the reinstatement of workers fired for union activity. Legal protections did not exclude any particular groups of workers. The government lacked the capacity to enforce applicable laws effectively.

Somali trade unions and the International Trade Union Confederation filed a legal complaint of violations of the Right to Organize and Collective Bargaining Convention and the Freedom of Association and Protection of the Right to Organize Convention at the International Labor Organization (ILO). The ILO Committee on Freedom of Association found the government responsible for violating freedom of association and trade union rights.

Government and employers respected freedom of association.

b. Prohibition of Forced or Compulsory Labor

The provisional federal constitution states a person may not be subjected to slavery, servitude, trafficking, or forced labor for any purpose. Authorities did not effectively enforce the law. Under the pre-1991 penal code, applicable at the federal and regional levels, the penalty for slavery is imprisonment for five to 20 years. The penalty for using forced labor is imprisonment for six months to five years. Although the penalties appeared sufficiently stringent, they were rarely applied. There were no known efforts by the government to prevent and eliminate forced labor in the country. The Ministry of Labor did not have an inspectorate and conducted no labor-related inspections.

Forced labor occurred. Children and minority clan members were reportedly used as porters to transport the mild narcotic khat (or "miraa"); in farming, animal herding, and crushing stones; and in construction. The use of child soldiers remained a problem (see section 1.g.). Al-Shabaab also forced persons in their camps to move to the countryside, reportedly to raise cash crops for the organization.

Also see the Department of State's *Trafficking in Persons Report* at www.state.gov/j/tip/rls/tiprpt/.

c. Prohibition of Child Labor and Minimum Age for Employment

It was unclear whether there was a minimum age for employment. The pre-1991 labor code prohibits child labor, provides a legal minimum age of 15 for most employment, prescribes different minimum ages for certain hazardous activities, and prohibits those under 18 from night work in the industrial, commercial, and agricultural sectors, apart from work that engages family members only. The provisional federal constitution states, "No child may perform work or provide services that are not suitable for the child's age or create a risk to the child's health or development in any way." The provisional federal constitution defines a child as any person less than 18 years of age.

The federal Ministries of Labor and of Social Affairs, Gender, and Family Affairs are responsible for enforcing child labor laws. The ministries, however, did not enforce these laws. Many of the laws related to the commercial exploitation of children are included in the 1962 penal code. These laws are not adequate to prevent child labor, as many of the fines have become negligible due to inflation. The government participated in campaigns to remove children from participation in armed conflict (see section 1.g.).

Child labor was widespread. The recruitment and use of child soldiers remained a problem. Youths commonly worked in herding, agriculture, and household labor from an early age. Children broke rocks into gravel and worked as vendors of cigarettes and khat on the streets. UNICEF estimated that, from 1999 to 2005, the latest date for which figures were available, 36 percent of children between the ages of five and 14 were in the workforce. Observers believed the actual percentage of working children to be higher.

Also see the Department of Labor's *Findings on the Worst Forms of Child Labor* at www.dol.gov/ilab/reports/child-labor/findings/.

d. Discrimination with Respect to Employment and Occupation

The law and regulations prohibit discrimination regarding race, sex, disability, political opinion, color, language, or social status, but the government did not effectively enforce those laws and regulations. Penalties were not sufficient to deter violations. The law does not prohibit discrimination on the basis of religion, age, or HIV-positive status.

The Somali Congress of Trade Unions stated the organization had received several complaints from job seekers of gender- and clan-based discrimination at the largest companies in the country but that authorities did not have the capacity to enforce antidiscrimination provisions.

e. Acceptable Conditions of Work

There was no national minimum wage.

The labor code requires equal pay for equal work. It provides for a standard workweek of 48 hours and at least nine paid national holidays and 15 days' annual leave, requires premium pay for overtime, and limits overtime to a maximum of 12 hours per week. The law sets occupational health and safety standards.

There was no organized effort to monitor working conditions. The Ministry of Labor was responsible at the federal level for enforcement, although it was not effective.

Wages and working conditions were established largely through ad hoc arrangements based on supply, demand, and the influence of workers' clans. There was no information on the existence or status of foreign or migrant workers in the country. Most workers worked in the informal sector.

Authorities did not have the capacity to effectively protect workers who wished to remove themselves from situations that endangered their health or safety, although no such cases were reported.